Celebrating the Name Anthony

Walter the Educator

Silent King Books

dedicated to everyone with the first name of Anthony

ANTHONY

In the realm of names, there's one that shines,

A beacon of strength, where greatness aligns.

Anthony, oh Anthony, your name rings true,

A symphony of power, in all that you do.

From ancient origins, it proudly stems,

A
N
T
H
O
N
Y

A name brimming with vigor, like precious gems.

With each letter, a story unfolds,

A tale of resilience, as history beholds.

A, the first letter, a mark of ascent,

Leading the way, with unwavering intent.

N, a noble sound, echoing through time,

A name of honor, in its prime.

T, a tower of determination and might,

Guiding the path, through day and night.

H, the heart of valor and grace,

A name of distinction, in every place.

O, the open sky, where dreams take flight,

A name that soars, in boundless height.

N, the never-ending spirit within,

A name of endurance, destined to win.

ANTHONY

Y, a yearning for all that's yet to be,

A name of possibility, wild and free.

Anthony, oh Anthony, a name to adore,

A

N

T

H

O

N

Y

In every syllable, it holds so much more.

A
N
T
H
O
N
Y

In tales of old and legends anew,

Your name echoes, strong and true.

In the annals of time, it leaves its mark,

A name of valor, lighting the dark.

In the fields of battle, it stands tall,

A name that answers the valiant call.

In the halls of wisdom, it seeks to learn,

A name that kindles the fires to burn.

Anthony, oh Anthony, a name to acclaim,

In every letter, it builds its fame.

From the whispers of history to the modern day,

Your name stands strong, in every way.

So here's to Anthony, in all his might,

A name that shines, in radiant light.

In every verse and in every story,

Your name stands tall, in all its glory.

From A to Y, it paints a tale,

A
N
T
H
O
N
Y

Of strength and courage that will prevail.

Anthony, oh Anthony, a name so grand,

In every word, it takes a stand.

May your name echo through the ages,

As a beacon of hope for all stages.

Anthony, oh Anthony, in every rhyme,

A
N
T
H
O
N
Y

Your name lives on, throughout all time.

ABOUT THE CREATOR

Walter the Educator is one of the pseudonyms for Walter Anderson. Formally educated in Chemistry, Business, and Education, he is an educator, an author, a diverse entrepreneur, and he is the son of a disabled war veteran. "Walter the Educator" shares his time between educating and creating. He holds interests and owns several creative projects that entertain, enlighten, enhance, and educate, hoping to inspire and motivate you.

Follow, find new works, and stay up to date
with Walter the Educator™
at WaltertheEducator.com